NEVER CALL
YOUR BROKER
ON MONDAY

NEVER CALL YOUR BROKER ON MONDAY

*And 300 Other Financial Lessons
You Can't Afford Not to Know*

NANCY DUNNAN

HarperPerennial
A Division of HarperCollins*Publishers*

HarperCollins books may be purchased for educational, business, or sales promotional use. For information, please write to: Special Markets Department, HarperCollins Publishers Inc., 10 East 53rd Street, New York, New York 10022.

Designed by Irving Perkins Associates

Library of Congress Cataloging-in-Publication Data
Dunnan, Nancy.
    Never call your broker on monday: and 300 other financial lessons you can't afford not to know / Nancy Dunnan. — 1st ed.
        p.   cm.
    ISBN 0-06-270164-9
    1. Finance, Personal—United States. 2. Investments—United States.
I. Title.
HG179.D863   1997
332.024—DC20   96-30186

97 98 99 00 01 ❖/HC 10 9 8 7 6 5 4 3 2

A fool and his money are soon parted.
AN ENGLISH PROVERB

ACKNOWLEDGMENTS

The author would like to thank five very special people who contributed their wit, wisdom, and time to this project:

Robert Wilson, my editor at HarperCollins, who conceived and fashioned the book and carefully shaped it into its final form;

Mitch Douglas, of International Creative Management, my agent; Julie Tripp, financial reporter at The Oregonian, who contributed her own expertise;

And Jay Pack and Samantha Biro, both of whom added to and improved each entry.

NO ONE will argue with the fact that information is a good thing. As Louis Pasteur said, "Chance favors the prepared mind."

Yet, when there's too much of a good thing, it becomes overwhelming, difficult to make a decision, and easier to ignore it all.

Nowhere is there more information available than in the area of personal finance. Each day we're bombarded with new insights about stocks, bonds, mutual funds, credit cards, real estate, loans, debts, insurance, banks, retirement plans, and other financial concerns.

This nonstop barrage of advice is delivered in various platforms:

books, newsletters, magazines, online services, radio, TV, newspapers, and even by so-called gurus. It invariably comes with a hidden (and sometimes not so hidden) message that here, at last, is "the" answer for how to get rich.

It would take you years to wade through all this stuff.

That's why I wrote such a simple book. After all, good advice is not based upon length, complex formulas, obscure theories, or esoteric data known only to a handful of people on Wall Street. Good advice is based on common sense, sound information, and proven techniques.

And because I know you're in a rush, I've made each of the lessons in this book as short, to the point, and uncomplicated as possible. I believe that if you easily grasp these concepts you're very likely to put them to work. Follow just a few and I promise that you'll either save money or make money, or both. Handle them as you would a vitamin: one a day. At the end of the year, you'll be in much better financial health.

Weigh Yourself.

DETERMINE YOUR net worth: Add up your assets (house, investments, car, insurance, collectibles) and subtract your liabilities (mortgage, credit card debt, loans). Strive to make your net worth increase every year.

Make a List of Financial Goals.

You'll feel great crossing them out.

— ¢ —

Invest in Interest Rates.

When U.S. interest rates are lower than foreign rates, invest in government bonds of foreign countries with stable governments and higher rates than ours.

Toss Out the Shoebox.

GET ORGANIZED. Buy a filing cabinet. Unless you know what you own, where it is, and how much it's worth, your financial life will be a muddle.

Find Your Money.

SET ASIDE one day a year to get your financial papers in order. Lost or missing financial documents can cost you or your family time and money.

Skip Mutual Funds with High Expense Ratios.

STOCK AND BOND FUNDS with expenses over 1.5% do little more than reduce your profits.

— ¢ —

Sell Items You Don't Need.

GET RID of the clutter. Have a garage sale. Invest the profits in a money market fund.

Always Be in the Highest Yielding Fund.

JUST ANY old money market fund won't do. Choose the best one. Financial magazines and the business section of the Sunday newspaper list the top yielding funds.

— ¢ —

Give It Away.

DONATE ITEMS you don't need to a charity. Get a written receipt. This is one of the few tax write-offs left for those who itemize their deductions.

Stick to an Allowance.

WHEN YOU run out, that's it. By limiting the amount of cash you spend on a weekly basis, you'll have more to invest.

—¢—

Don't Bank on Your Bank.

THE INTEREST on bank savings accounts doesn't even keep up with inflation. Move your savings to a money market fund. You'll nearly double your return. This can be accomplished with just two phone calls—one to your bank, one to your mutual fund.

Use Your Money Market Fund as a Checking Account.

BANKS CHARGE for checks. Money market funds don't.

— ¢ —

Pretend That This Year Is Your Last Year of Work.

YOU'LL SAVE more money, spend less, and tackle retirement planning issues in earnest.

Buy a CD That Doesn't Send You Interest Until Maturity.

YOU'LL BENEFIT from compounding. Otherwise, request that your bank automatically invest the interest in your money market or savings account.

Put Savings on Automatic Pilot.

YOU CAN'T spend what you can't touch, so sign up for an automatic savings plan at work. Have your employer deposit part of your check into a mutual fund, or have the fund take a preset amount from your checking account each pay period.

Save.

IF YOU put aside just $25 a week, at the end of the year you'll have $1,300, plus interest. This is enough to get you into a money market fund.

Don't Shortchange Your IRA.

IF YOU invest the maximum allowed each year—$2,000—and you're in the 28% tax bracket, in ten years you'll have almost $30,000, assuming it earns 7% annually. In 30 years, that's $202,146. In a taxable investment, those figures would only be $26,473 and $140,537, respectively.

Buy CDs Through a Stockbroker.

BROKERAGE FIRMS shop the nation's banks, getting much higher rates than those offered by individual banks.

Go for Plain Vanilla.

INVESTING IN EE Savings Bonds is ultra safe. There's no fee to buy or redeem them, and you'll never have to pay state or local taxes on the interest earned. If you're a beginner, start with just $25 at your local bank or through payroll deduction where you work.

"*Never Invest Your Money in Anything That Eats or Needs Repainting.*"

SO SAID Broadway producer Billy Rose. If you follow his advice, you are basically left with the stock market. Not a bad thing. Over the past 20 years, stocks have consistently had a better return than Treasuries.

Go with What You Know.

BUY STOCK in the company you work for—unless it's not financially solid. You know as well as anyone on Wall Street how well it's run. It's an easy way to get into the market. But don't overdo it. Every company has its ups and downs.

— ¢ —

Invest in Vanity.

BUY STOCKS in high-profile companies whose products are designed to make you feel good and look good.

Learn to Earn.

DUMMIES DON'T make money, so sign up for a course in personal finance. Skip the free seminars—they're usually a way for the sponsor to find new clients.

—¢—

Take Notes.

KEEP A FINANCIAL notebook. Jot down any smart tips you come upon. Like good gloves, umbrellas, and sunglasses, good ideas have a way of getting lost.

Read the Business Section of a Newspaper at Least Once a Week.

WITHIN A MONTH you'll know a lot more about the stock market, interest rates, the economy, and financial trends.

— ¢ —

Leave Advice for the Masses to the Masses.

INVESTMENT TIPS on radio and TV are heard by you—and everyone else listening. That doesn't mean they're not valid—just that you won't be getting in on the ground floor.

Be an Investment Groupie.

FOR ABOUT $35 a month you can belong to an investment club, learn about the market, and buy stocks with friends. Organizations like the Michigan-based National Association of Investment Clubs can help you get started.

Set Up Your Investment Club as a Partnership, Not a Corporation.

A CORPORATION pays taxes, a partnership doesn't. Partners are responsible for paying taxes only on their share of the club's income.

Play in Your Own Backyard.

IF YOUR public utility is financially solid and pays a high dividend, buy shares. Many let customers purchase their first shares directly from the company, bypassing a stockbroker. Contact the utility's investor relations department for details.

Go for Household Names.

INVEST IN companies that make well-known, brand-name products. Consumers generally choose them over the competition. (Hint: Listen to your kids. They'll probably know what's hot before you do.)

Avoid Greed and Fear.

THESE ARE the investor's Achilles heels. Keeping all your money in the bank earning 3% interest is just as foolish as dumping your entire savings into the market thinking you'll make a quick buck.

Check Out Your Broker.

WATCHDOG GROUPS—such as the Better Business Bureau, your State Attorney General's Office, and the National Association of Securities Dealers in Gaithersburg, Maryland—can tell you if any complaints or legal actions have been filed against a broker you're considering.

Don't Hire a Relative.

PAYING YOUR cousin to manage your finances, do your tax return, or pick your stocks is bound to lead to trouble. Separate family and finances.

Give a Cold Shoulder to Cold Callers.

NEVER INVEST in anything based on a phone call from someone you don't know or whose office is a post office box.

Sleep on It.

NEVER BUY an investment the first day
you hear about it. Think about it
overnight. Impulse investments—like
impulse romances—can come back
to haunt you.

Don't Collar Your Broker Out of the Office.

NEVER DISCUSS your account with your broker at a party, in an elevator, or if he's headed out the door. The same with financial planners and accountants. They can't give you their undivided attention while sipping martinis, looking for the right floor button, or putting on their coats.

— ¢ —

Read What Your Broker Reads.

IF YOU don't know what your stockbroker reads, ask.

Do Your Own Research.

EVEN THE smartest broker in town can't possibly know everything. So, read company annual and quarterly reports, brokerage firm studies, and investment newsletters.

— ¢ —

Spend Three Minutes Planning Your Call to a Stockbroker.

KNOW WHAT you want to accomplish before you place the call. Good brokers are very busy, especially during market hours.

*Never Invest in Anything Until
You Have Three Good Reasons.*

Invest Less at the End of the Month.

BROKERS TEND to push stocks at the end of the month in an effort to match or surpass their previous month's sales.

Use Stop Orders.

PROTECT YOUR profits. Stop orders direct your broker to sell a security if it drops or climbs to a particular price. For example, if you purchase a stock at $20 per share and it moves up to $35, guarantee yourself a profit by putting in a stop order to sell the stock if it falls to $30—or if it rises to $40.

Always Leave a Sinking Ship.

THERE'S NO virtue in hanging on to losers. And stocks don't have feelings.

— ¢ —

Don't Rely on the Internet.

THE INTERNET may deliver information fast, but it can't pick stocks. You still need to think. You still need a broker who can think.

Never Fire Your Broker by Voice- or E-mail.

BE COURTEOUS. Deliver the bad news in a phone conversation or in person and do everything possible to remain on good terms. You may need your broker's help in the future—for things like back records and tax information.

Never Confuse Income with Growth.

ALWAYS KNOW whether you're investing for income (money market funds, CDs, savings accounts, bonds, high-dividend stocks) or appreciation (growth stocks and mutual funds, real estate, collectibles, precious metals, antiques). If you confuse the two, you might sell assets that grow in price (because they don't produce dividends) or sell income producers (because they don't go up in price). This is no way to make money.

Understand the Pros and Cons of Risk.

THE RISKIER an investment, the greater the potential for a tremendous return or a tremendous loss.

— ¢ —

Make Financial Decisions When You're Sharpest.

IN THE morning, at night, after a nap, with a cup of coffee, on the weekend.

Read the Fine Print.

DON'T OVERLOOK the fine print in a prospectus, brokerage account agreement, insurance policy, annuity, or retirement plan. It's boring—but revealing. If you don't understand it, hire someone who does.

Use the "Kiss" Plan.

"KEEP IT simple, stupid" was the basic philosophy of billionaire Ray Kroc, founder of McDonald's. Don't own so many investments that you can't keep track of them. Five stocks are fine, ten are plenty. If you're rich enough to own more, pay someone else to watch your investments for you. And instruct them to follow the "kiss" plan.

Don't Confuse "Government" with "Safe."

SOME MUTUAL funds use "government" in their name. But Treasuries, Ginnie Maes, and government agency issues, just like other investments, rise and fall in value.

Find a Broker Who Is Above Reproach.

DON'T HAVE anyone on your financial team with whom you wouldn't trust your mother's money or your kid's life.

Dive into the Dow.

ONCE A YEAR, invest equal dollar amounts in the ten highest yielding stocks in the Dow Jones Industrial Average. Also, once a year, replace those that no longer rank in the top ten with those that do. The thirty stocks in the Dow are listed every day in the *Wall Street Journal.* This technique has beaten the overall return on the DJIA since 1972.

Buy a Cash Cow.

THE MORE cash a company has on hand, the better it is able to weather economic slowdowns and to buy other companies at bargain prices without having to borrow.

Aim Low.

GO FOR solid companies with low P/Es. The P/E ratio is a company's stock price divided by the 12-month earnings per share. Stocks with low P/Es often outperform the market, although there are no guarantees. P/Es are listed in the stock tables.

Use a Discount Broker.

IF YOU know the stocks and bonds you want to buy, purchase them through a discount broker instead of a full-service broker. You'll save from 50% to 75% in commissions.

Go for the Index.

NO-LOAD INDEX mutual funds make experts of us all. These funds invest in a representative basket of stocks of a particular index—such as the Standard & Poor's 500 Index—and their returns mirror that index. It's a no-brainer way to at least keep pace with the market, and often to make a lot of money. Three-quarters of all professional money managers do not outperform the S&P 500 Index on a regular basis.

Listen to the Chairman.

THE CHAIRMAN of the Federal Reserve reports to Congress every six months on the state of the economy. If he predicts that inflation is easing off, buy bonds and longer-term Treasuries to lock in current yields. If inflation is heating up, buy big ticket items before prices rise further.

Go with Puerto Rico.

PUERTO RICO'S municipal bonds are exempt from federal and state income taxes in all fifty states.

— ¢ —

Cash In on a Lower Trade Deficit.

WHEN THE trade deficit is low, the dollar is strong and foreign investors eagerly buy U.S. Treasuries. At this point, add Treasury notes and bonds to your portfolio in order to lock in high yields.

Keep Your Broker in the Loop.

IF A CHANGE in your personal life changes your financial situation, tell your broker.

Wait for January.

IN THIRTY-SIX out of forty-five years since 1950, as January went, so went the market. If Wall Street likes the President's annual State of the Union message and federal budget for the coming year, investor enthusiasm tends to buoy the market for the next twelve months.

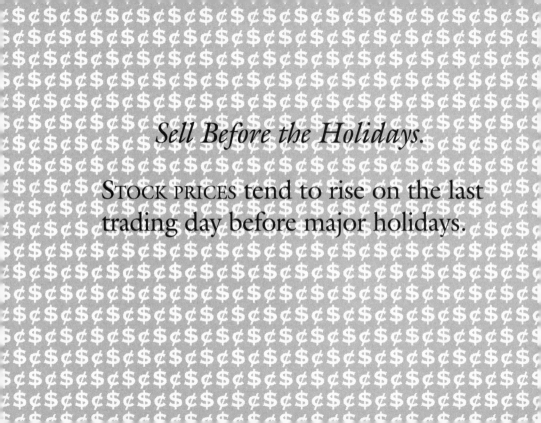

Sell Before the Holidays.

STOCK PRICES tend to rise on the last trading day before major holidays.

Trade During the Holidays.

THE STOCK market often moves up during the week between Christmas and New Year's Day as money managers sell stocks that were losers during the year and buy new ones before clients do their end-of-the-year portfolio review.

Don't Be Afraid of Heights.

INVEST IN companies with high profit margins. A firm's profit margin (earnings divided by revenues) indicates that management is keeping costs in rein. Check out the annual report—or call the company for the figure.

Don't Sell a Stock Until a Few Days After It Goes Ex-Dividend.

THAT WAY you get to keep the dividend. The buyer of a stock selling ex-dividend does not receive the most recently declared dividend; that dividend goes to the seller. For example, if GE goes ex-dividend on June 31, an investor buying the stock on or after that date will not receive the latest declared dividend when it's paid.

Buy Spinoff Companies.

SPINOFFS GO up in price after being sold off by their parent company because they are almost always run by managers who understand the business and know where to cut costs. About 14% of spinoffs also become takeover targets, which likewise boosts the price of the stock.

Be Nice to Your Broker.

EVERY BROKER makes mistakes. If your broker makes too many, simply look for a new one.

— ¢ —

Buy Stocks After They Split.

STOCKS OFTEN rise in price on news of a split and fall right after the split. Wait and take advantage of the lower price. (A stock split is a division of shares, frequently 2-for-1. Splits usually occur when the price of a stock has risen so high that investors are reluctant to buy it.)

Purchase Buybacks.

WHEN A CORPORATION goes into the marketplace to buy back its own stock, it means management thinks the stock is undervalued. This is a smart time to buy.

Bet on Black.

BUY LOW-DEBT or no-debt companies. When the economy is in trouble, these companies usually have enough cash on hand to stay out of trouble. And they seldom need to borrow when interest rates are high.

— ¢ —

Beware of Very High Yields.

THE HIGHER the yield, the higher the risk. A high yield is designed to attract investors. An outrageously high yield attracts fools.

Follow Insider Trading.

WHEN CORPORATE executives buy or sell shares in their own company it means they know something that you don't. Financial magazines and newspapers report this trading activity on a regular basis.

Get a Biannual Checkup.

REVIEW YOUR investments twice a year. Unload losers—those that have dropped in price 10% or more over six months. Add to the winners—those that have moved up 8% or more. Replace losers with promising newcomers.

Know Your Returns.

DON'T LEAVE it to chance or up to your broker. Take the current value of your investment (the price of a stock or net asset value of a mutual fund), subtract its value from a year ago, and divide the result by the value of a year ago. That's your return for the year. For example: If your mutual fund holding was worth $1,000 a year ago and today it's worth $1,500, your return is 50% ($1,500 minus $1,000, divided by $1,000). Compare that with the return on the S&P 500.

Never Fall in Love with an Investment.

KEEP DECISIONS about buying and selling rational: Sell losers and keep winners.

— ¢ —

Don't Be Ignorant.

NEVER BUY a stock without first knowing what business the company is in.

Get on the College Acceleration Plan.

OVER 150 U.S. colleges award four-year degrees in three years. This can cut the total cost of a B.S. by up to $20,000, including room and board.

— ¢ —

Boast Not, Want Not.

EGO HAS no place in investment decisions. Bragging about your winners may ultimately get in the way of clear thinking.

Sell Your Losers.

LOOK OUT for a sudden drop. When the price of a stock falls 20% from its high, sell. It's probably a sign of trouble. This no-brainer strategy limits losses and takes emotion out of the decision-making process.

Don't Be a Pig.

BULLS MAKE money and bears make money, but pigs seldom do. When a stock or mutual fund is up 30%, sell one-quarter of your position.

Sell Your Winners.

WHEN YOUR favorite stock is in the news and making new highs, sell at least one-quarter your position. Stash the money in T-bills or a money market fund until a new investment opportunity comes along.

Sell When Interest Rates Head North.

ESCALATING RATES push stock prices down because investors move out of stocks and into CDs, money market funds, and bonds. Take profits in stocks when the 3-month Treasury Bill rate moves up several times within a couple of months, or when the Fed raises short-term interest rates twice within twelve months.

— ¢ —

Don't Be Fooled by Bells and Whistles.

AVOID MAKING investment decisions based on elaborate flow charts, multicolored graphs, and the babble of analysts.

— ¢ —

Choose a Stock Based on Four Factors.

THEY ARE: 1) earnings; 2) debt level; 3) management style; and 4) the value of its product or service in the marketplace.

Watch the Gross Domestic Product.

WHEN THE Gross Domestic Product is increasing 3% to 5% a year, buy solid growth stocks. These, too, will increase—in price.

Avoid the Nanny Tax.

TAKE YOUR child to day care instead of hiring an in-home nanny, and hire a cleaning service rather than a maid. You won't have to pay Social Security taxes because the IRS considers these employees independent contractors, not household help.

Track Durable Goods.

WHEN ORDERS for durable goods are up several months in a row, buy stock in manufacturers of durable goods. (A durable good is a product with a long shelf life, such as appliances, cars, and furniture.) When orders are flat or down, buy stocks in recession-resistant companies—those that manufacture products such as food and beverages.

Keep an Eye on the Producer Price Index.

WHEN THE Producer Price Index moves up several percentage points, interest rates will also rise because the Fed will tighten money in order to keep a lid on inflation. Be ready to buy longer-term CDs, bonds, and Treasuries just as rates start to move up.

Employ the Unemployment Rate.

WHEN THE unemployment rate is above 6% the Fed will start to lower interest rates. Lock in yields on CDs and bonds before rates fall any further.

Make Business Your Business.

WHEN NEW business starts are up, the economy is in good shape, so move out of money market funds and CDs and into growth stocks. When business failures are up, interest rates tend to be high and the economy will start to decline. Lock in yields on CDs, Treasuries, and A-rated corporate bonds and move into recession-resistant stocks, such as food, beverages, drugs, and utilities.

Look to the Third World.

INVEST IN countries with the lowest unit labor costs. They attract new businesses. Purchase shares in a single country mutual fund or closed-end country stock fund. (Caution: Use only money earmarked for high risk.)

— ¢ —

Apply for a Loan When Interest Rates Fall.

LOANS AND mortgages cost less, and rates will eventually go back up.

Buy Stock in Companies That Make Big Ticket Items When Interest Rates Are Low.

LOW RATES encourage the use of credit and the purchase of homes, automobiles, land, boats, and furniture.

Take Note When Auto Sales Start to Rise.

THIS IS the time to buy stocks in auto and tire companies, as well as manufacturers of glass, rubber, and steel, provided the companies are well managed and have strong balance sheets. When auto sales peak, sell.

Follow Housing Starts.

WHEN THEY are up, invest in cement, glass, lumber, furniture, carpeting, household appliances, and home builders and manufacturers. Buy at least one REIT (real estate investment trust).

Catch the Wave.

WHEN INTEREST rates start to rise, take out a loan or mortgage before they climb higher. This is also a good time to refinance your mortgage.

— ¢ —

Lock in Yields When Rates Are High.

WHEN INTEREST rates are high, lock in yields on long-term CDs, Treasuries, and bonds. Rates will eventually fall.

Go Multinational.

INVEST IN U.S. multinational corporations when the dollar is down. A lower dollar makes the cost of American exports cheaper to foreign consumers. Multinational corporations—those that receive 30% or more of their revenues from foreign countries— thrive when the dollar is weak.

Invest in Inflation.

As WILL Rogers once said, "It's the only thing going up." Buy inflation-resistant stocks: drugs, cosmetics, medicine, food, beverages, public utilities, health care. Stocks in companies that make wine, liquor, and other beverages also fare well in the face of inflation.

Let Your Fingers Do the Walking.

LOOK UP telephone numbers yourself. Use information twice a day every day of the year, at 45 cents per inquiry and you're spending $338 annually. Add on the automatic dialing service at 35 cents per call and you're looking at close to $256 per year. Combine the two and you're giving your phone company nearly $600 a year.

Diversify.

"BUSINESS WILL be better or worse," Calvin Coolidge once told a group of eminent economists. So diversify among various industries to protect yourself against those businesses doing worse. The same principle holds true for mutual funds.

Wait to Buy a Closed-end Fund.

WHEN FIRST offered to the public, the price of a closed-end fund includes an underwriting fee of around 6%. Three to six months later most sell for about 15% less. (A closed-end fund invests in a variety of securities and trades on a stock exchange.)

Don't Be an Odd Duck.

BUY STOCKS in round lots of 100 shares to save on brokerage commissions. Brokers charge the same commission for 40 as for 100 shares.

Join Your Kids at College.

PARENTS ENROLLED for six credits in a college degree program may be considered full-time students. The more full-time students in one family the more likely someone in the family will be awarded financial aid.

Sign Up for a DRIP.

MANY CORPORATIONS offer DRIPs (Dividend Reinvestment Plans) in which shareholders can automatically reinvest their dividends in more shares and not pay a brokerage commission. With most DRIPs, you can also make additional cash purchases of shares, either commission-free or for a nominal amount. (For information about DRIPs, call the company itself or consult Standard & Poor's *Dividend Reinvestment Directory,* published annually.)

— ¢ —

Write Off Your Investment Expenses.

IF YOU itemize your tax deductions, many investment expenses are deductible. These include: subscriptions to investment publications, safe deposit box rentals, transportation to meet with your broker or accountant, fees charged by investment advisors—and this book.

Pay Attention to Discomfort.

IF YOU'RE uncomfortable with your financial advisor, it's probably with good reason.

Know Your Investment.

DON'T THINK you can make money
investing in wine, gold coins, oil, or
cattle unless you know something
about wine, gold coins, oil, or cattle.

Beware When No-load Is a Load.

ALTHOUGH "NO-LOAD" funds don't charge you to buy or sell shares, some have annual 12b–1 fees to cover promotional costs. Switch out of a fund with a 12b–1 fee higher than 0.25% of its assets.

Hold the Line.

INVEST THE same dollar amount every month in the same mutual fund. You'll wind up buying more shares when prices are low and fewer when prices are high. This also works for stocks. In both cases, dollar cost averaging reduces the average price of your shares. And you don't have to worry about trying to time the market—something even the experts don't do very well.

Double-check the Check.

ALWAYS ADD up the restaurant tab. Miscalculations are usually in the restaurant's favor, not yours.

$$-\cent-$$

Reinvest.

ALL MUTUAL funds let you automatically reinvest earned income in additional shares. Sign on. You can't spend what you don't get your hands on.

Limit the Number of Mutual Funds You Own.

THE AVERAGE investor needs five at the most: a money market fund, a growth fund, a growth and income fund, a small company fund, and an international fund.

Never Buy Mutual Funds Just Before Distribution Time.

BEFORE INVESTING in a fund or buying additional shares in one you already own, call the company and ask when the next distribution date will be. Then, buy after the distribution. Otherwise, you'll wind up paying taxes on any capital gains, dividend, or interest income the fund earned before you bought your shares. For example, you buy a mutual fund at $20 per share on December 1st. On December 15th the fund distributes capital gains of $1.50 per share and 50 cents per share in dividends. The Net Asset Value (NAV) drops to $18 per share and yet, as a new investor, you have to pay income tax on the $2 distribution.

– ¢ –

Invest in Success.

MAKE A LIST of companies that turn out the best cereal, candy, batteries, soft drinks, washing machines, automobiles, bicycles, laptop computers. Good products make for good investments.

Save Your Next Raise or Bonus.

YOU WERE managing fine without it. Have it automatically deducted from your paycheck, or from your checking account, and invest it in a money market or growth stock fund.

— ¢ —

Take Your Broker to Lunch.

AT LEAST once a year, and be sure to pick up the tab.

Buy the Least Expensive House in an Expensive Neighborhood.

IT WILL be much easier to sell than the most expensive house in an inexpensive neighborhood.

Save What You Were Paying on a Loan.

WHEN YOU pay off your mortgage, a car, credit card, or college loan, put that same dollar amount into savings. You were living without it; now regard it as "found" money.

— ¢ —

Pay Yourself Second.

AFTER WRITING your rent or mortgage check, make the next one out for savings. Begin saving 1% of your take-home pay and increase it by 1% each month. By the end of a year you'll be saving a respectable 12%.

Visit Your ATM Just Once a Week.

FIGURE OUT how much cash you'll need to get through seven days. Take it out on Monday morning and don't go back until the same time next week. You'll save on bank fees and probably spend less.

Make Sure Your Money Is Insured.

FDIC INSURANCE covers up to $100,000 per bank account. If you have $200,000 in savings and checking combined, it's considered as one account and insured up to just $100,000. (An IRA is considered a second account and insured separately, also up to $100,000.) Do business with more than one bank if your account exceeds $100,000.

Cut Up All Credit Cards but One.

PAYING WITH cash or by check is a surefire way to spend less, reduce debt, and have more to invest. And, unless you're frequently traveling, leave that one card at home.

— ¢ —

Travel Lightly.

PUT SEVERAL traveler's checks in your wallet to cover emergencies instead of credit cards or a wad of bills. A wallet bulging with cash is a wallet asking to be emptied.

Leave Your Checkbook at Home.

AVOID TEMPTATION: Carry just one check.

Negotiate for a Cash Discount.

RETAILERS, RESTAURANTS, and hotels pay 2% to 5% to the credit card company when you use your card. If you pay cash, bargain for a discount.

Go Local.

INVEST IN a publicly traded corporation headquartered in your backyard. You're likely to know how financially stable it is. Buy shares if it is well managed and steer clear of any corporation facing strikes, legal problems, plant closings, or falling earnings. Read your local newspaper to keep up-to-date. Check with a local stockbroker to confirm your hunch.

Switch to a Secured Credit Card If You're Plastic Happy.

YOU'LL AVOID overspending with this type of card since you can only charge up to the dollar amount in your bank account.

Challenge Your Property Taxes.

ABOUT 60% of all homeowners pay more than they should. Assessment mistakes are common and real estate values do drop. Educate yourself—find out what houses similar to yours are worth—or consult a lawyer who specializes in property taxes. (If you're 65 or older, ask for a tax abatement or to have taxes deferred until after your house is sold.)

Use a Prepaid Telephone Card.

IT'S OFTEN the cheapest way to make brief (three minutes or less) long distance calls.

— ¢ —

Refinance Your Mortgage When Interest Rates Are Low.

FOLLOW THIS rule of thumb: Refinance only if you can reduce your rate by at least 2%. Otherwise, any savings is eaten up by fees for the application, appraisal, title insurance, and other legal stuff.

Limit Drinking at Restaurants.

ALCOHOLIC BEVERAGES are the profit center for restaurants. Don't confuse dining out with a keg party.

Take the $125,000 Tax Exemption.

IF YOU'RE over age 55, you can get a once-in-a-lifetime exclusion for up to $125,000 of gain on the sale of your primary residence—if it's been your residence for three of the five previous years. (Only one exclusion is allowed per married couple. If your spouse used the exclusion, even when he/she was not married to you, you're out of luck.) If you've never used the exclusion and you're going to get married to someone who has used it, sell your house before tying the knot.

Pay Off Your Highest Interest Debt First.

EACH WEEK, put something—even $10 or $20—toward your credit card loan with the highest interest rate, not the largest amount due. Then, move onto the next highest.

Turn Talent Into Cash.

NEVER GIVE it away. Get paid for what you like doing—babysitting, carpentry, catering, consulting, cooking, editing, gardening, makeup, number crunching, painting, sewing, wallpapering, word processing, writing.

Never Pay If You Don't Have To.

BARTER YOUR services or goods for something you need—free garage space for car repairs, accounting skills for secretarial work, word processing for hair cuts, reduced rent for doing repairs, free room and board for child care.

Consolidate Your Finances.

IF YOU'RE paying annual or monthly fees on several accounts, put them at one bank and/or one brokerage firm. You'll save money and be better able to manage your finances with everything summarized on one monthly statement.

Remember Your Net Worth.

USE IT to determine the appropriate risk level for all your investments. If your net worth is over $1 million, buy an umbrella liability insurance policy to protect your assets in the event you're the target of a lawsuit. Just $300 gets you $1 million in coverage.

*Never Confuse Investing
with Speculation.*

BOTH MAY have a place in your
portfolio, but know which is which.

Stop to Think and Think to Stop.

THINK THROUGH all your financial decisions—from buying a house to building a portfolio—and learn when to stop and change direction.

$-¢-$

Don't Follow the Crowd.

IF EVERYONE is buying, it's no longer a bargain.

Paddle Your Own Canoe.

HAVE THE courage of your own
convictions and don't be swayed
by friends who boast about their
financial home runs. Last year's
winners are often this year's losers.

Don't Try to Keep Up with the Joneses.

HUNDREDS OF Joneses are so busy buying things that they can't keep up with their own bills. They are among the 1.6 million Americans who declare personal bankruptcy each year. Don't be one of them.

Invest in Your Bank.

IF YOUR bank is financially healthy and publicly traded, buy shares. As a stockholder you may get special treatment, such as no-minimum balance checking accounts, lower fees, free checking, better loan consideration. Check first with the branch manager or corporate headquarters to make sure.

Hire Your Kids.

IF YOU'RE self-employed, put your kids on the payroll and deduct their salaries as a business expense. This not only teaches them responsibility, but also gives them some spending money and you a tax break.

Don't Give Cash to Your Charity.

INSTEAD OF cash, donate stocks, property, antiques, paintings, and other appreciated assets, and take a tax deduction for their market value. If they've appreciated in value, you'll avoid being hit with a capital gains tax.

— ¢ —

Don't Be Seduced by Sales.

BUYING ON sale is not saving. It's still spending.

Counter Counterfeiting.

IF YOU receive a fake bill, you're out of luck. Be smart and reject bills with corners cut off or taped back on. These are typical counterfeit ploys. If you need new bills for tips or presents, get them at your bank and not from a liquor store, supermarket, gas station, or convenience store—places where counterfeiters pass their wares.

Don't Choose Bond Mutual Funds for Fixed Income.

CONTRARY TO what many people think, funds do not hold on to bonds until they mature. A fund's yield varies continually as the manager buys and sells securities. If you want a guaranteed, fixed income, purchase individual A-rated corporate bonds or Treasuries and hold them until maturity.

Learn the Buzz Words.

WATCH THE business news at least once a week, with your financial notebook at your side.

Don't Compare Apples and Oranges.

SIMPLE INTEREST is not the same as the annual effective yield. Simple interest is the annual percentage rate without compounding. The annual effective yield is the return after compounding. (For example, a one-year 5% CD has a simple yield of 5% and an annual effective yield of 5.13%.) When picking a CD, money market fund, or savings account, compare the same figures.

Protect Your Financial Records Against Hell and High Water.

PUT TOGETHER an emergency fireproof file box. Stock it with the following: some cash and traveler's checks, insurance policies, passports, social security cards, your lease or deed, immunization records, bank and credit card numbers, checkbook, inventory of household possessions with photos or videotape, important telephone numbers, family records, copies of your will, birth, marriage, divorce, and death certificates, insurance policies, automobile registration, and copies of state and federal tax returns. Grab it in the event of a natural disaster.

Don't Play Noah.

BUY FLOOD insurance. Because your town has never experienced a flood doesn't mean that it never will. People in flood plain areas are 26 times more likely to have a flood than a fire during their 30-year mortgage period.

Keep Rolling.

WHEN YOUR EE Savings Bonds mature, roll them over into HH Bonds. You'll be able to delay paying federal income taxes until the HH bonds mature and until then, you'll earn 4% annually.

Use a Low Interest Rate Credit Card If You Don't Pay Your Bill in Full Every Month.

INTEREST NEVER sleeps.

— ¢ —

Use a No Annual Fee Card If You Pay Your Bill in Full Every Month.

FINANCIAL MAGAZINES run updated lists with telephone numbers.

129

Invest If It Will Play in Peoria.

PRODUCTS AND services that appeal to tiny segments of the population are a lot less likely to make outstanding investments than those with wide, universal appeal. If it works in Middle America, it will work everywhere else.

Pay Attention to the Numbers.

THEY DON'T lie. Check out the sales, earnings, and profits of a company before purchasing its stock or bonds. Numbers are the most unbiased, unemotional predictors of a company's future you'll find.

— ¢ —

Think Long Term.

IF YOU'RE looking for growth, hold on to an investment for at least four years.

Ask for a Report Card.

FEDERAL LAW requires companies and unions to give employees and members an annual written summary detailing the financial state of pension plans—what your money is invested in and how well it is doing. Compare its annual return with a benchmark such as the S&P 500 or the Dow Jones Industrial Average.

Pick Just One PIN.

USE THE same Personal Identification Number for all bank accounts, but never write it down. It must be easy for you to remember—but not obvious to anyone else. Skip your birthdate, phone number, or Social Security number. Instead, use your wedding anniversary, height, or salary.

Prioritize Your 401(k) Funding.

IF YOU and your spouse each have a 401(k), but you can only fund one to the max, pick the better of the two—the one that has a matching contribution from the employer, the most investment choices, and the better return.

— ¢ —

Recognize Temptation.

MAKE A LIST of your financial vulnerabilities. Review it from time to time and strive not to repeat your mistakes.

Never Shop with a Big Spender.

OR WITH a friend who is a bigger spender than you.

Get Fees in Writing—
Before Doing Business.

FEE-ONLY planners take a flat fee or a percentage of your assets and have less incentive to sell you products. Fee-based planners take both an up-front fee and a commission on trades.

Drive Like the Little Old Lady from Pasadena.

TELL YOUR auto insurance company that you have a safe driving record, and you may receive a premium reduction. This also works for nonsmokers, nondrinkers, driver ed grads, and those who install anti-theft devices in their vehicles.

Keep It in the Family.

BUYING YOUR auto, life, home, health, and disability insurance from the same company gives you plenty of leverage to negotiate really big discounts.

Never Be Rushed Into an Investment.

IF YOU are, something's wrong.
No good deal disappears overnight.

Beware When Banks Merge.

FDIC INSURANCE covers bank accounts up to $100,000 at any one institution. If you have accounts at two banks that merge, only $100,000 will be protected after six months. Move $100,000 to another bank or open another account in the same bank but in the name of another person in your family.

Give Children Savings Bonds, Not Cash.

EE BONDS can't be cashed in for six months and they teach kids the value of investing for the future. Seeing is believing: Be sure to show them the actual bonds.

Pay for Fender-benders Yourself.

RAISE YOUR auto insurance deductible from $100 to $500 and you'll save 10% to 15% on your premium. Boost it to $1,000 and you'll save as much as 30%.

Name a Second Beneficiary for Your IRA.

IF YOUR primary beneficiary does not outlive you, your retirement account will fall into your estate and subsequently be subject to legal fees and claims by any creditors. This could mean less for your heirs.

Beware of the Once-in-a-Lifetime Deal.

IF YOU think it's too good to be true, it probably is.

*Never Give Any Single Broker
Too Much of Your Money.*

PUTTING ALL your eggs in one basket
has been the downfall of many.

Don't Keep Cash in Your Safe Deposit Box.

IF IT'S stolen it's impossible to prove that it was there, so it won't be covered by insurance. Keep currency in a fireproof safe at home or locked away in your office.

— ¢ —

Don't Take Too Much Out of Your IRA.

THE MAXIMUM you can withdraw annually once you've reached age 70½ is currently $150,000. Exceed that amount and you'll be slapped with a 15% tax for excess distributions.

Negotiate with Your Broker.

IF YOU'RE a good customer, your broker may give you a break on commissions. The more money you have, the more likely this will happen. It definitely won't happen unless you ask.

Never Personally Accept Your Vested Retirement Savings.

WHEN YOU switch jobs, ask your previous employer to deposit your retirement savings directly in a rollover IRA or your new company's plan. If the distribution check is made out to you, your former employer must deduct 20% for taxes.

Avoid Early Retirement Withdrawals.

TAKING OUT money from a qualified retirement plan—before you're 59½—means paying a 10% penalty plus tax. Exception: If you're taking it in equal installments from an IRA.

Keep Municipal Bonds Out of Your IRA, Keogh, or SEP.

BECAUSE THE income from these bonds is tax-exempt, the yields are lower than on taxable bonds. Anything you put in your IRA is automatically sheltered from taxes, so go for higher yielding corporate bonds.

Value Average to Buy Low and Sell High.

INVEST TO increase your portfolio's value by a set dollar amount each month. For example, if you want your portfolio to increase by $250 each month, and it goes up $100 along with the market, add just $150. If it goes down $100, you need to put in $350.

Give Every Man Your Ear but None Your Purse.

FOLLOW SHAKESPEARE'S advice. Listen to the media, your broker, and to tipsters, but always make up your own mind.

$$-¢-$$

Think Durable.

DRAW UP a durable power of attorney that appoints someone to run your finances if you become incapacitated. If you don't, the court—not you—will decide who will handle things.

Diversify.

TO DETERMINE how much you should have in bonds, multiply your age by 75%. Divide that among corporates, Treasuries, and municipals. If you're 45, it will be approximately 33%. Put the rest in stocks.

Insure Your Future.

BUY ENOUGH life and disability insurance to cover five to seven times your yearly spending (not your annual income), including what you pay in taxes. If you have young children, add enough to pay off your mortgage and their college expenses.

— ¢ —

Know When to Unload a Mutual Fund.

SELL WHEN it has underperformed the average for funds in its category for 13 consecutive months. Categories include: growth, income, balanced, international, small cap, and sector.

Use a Small Bank.

You'll GET personalized attention, kinder service, and better rates. The lines will also be shorter.

Join a Credit Union.

THEY PAY higher rates on savings accounts, charge less for loans, have lower service fees, and work harder to help customers than most banks do.

Ignore the Self-congratulatory Stuff in a Company's Annual Report.

INSTEAD, SUBTRACT current liabilities from current assets to find out if there's enough capital to keep the firm afloat. Then, divide current assets by current liabilities to get the current ratio. A two-to-one ratio is okay for manufacturers. Less than that means trouble.

Get Garage Sale Protection.

BEFORE GIVING one, be sure your homeowner's insurance protects you if a stranger has an accident on your property.

— ¢ —

Make the First Move.

AVOID AN income gap: Apply for Social Security benefits at least
three months before retiring. The government has never been
known to move with lightning speed.

Monitor on a Monthly Basis.

FOLLOWING STOCK, bond and mutual fund prices every day will cloud your long-term vision, engender panic, and lead to emotional buy and sell decisions. Just look once every thirty days.

If You Have Seven Credit Cards, Get Rid of Three.

TOO MANY cards may make getting a mortgage or home equity loan more difficult. Lenders may think you have access to too much credit, heightening your potential for being overextended.

Ladder Your Treasuries.

BUY NOTES and bonds with differing maturity dates, i.e., one, three, five, and seven years. Reinvest as each comes due—in new ones if interest rates are high, in the stock market if rates are low.

Equate Co-Signing with Co-Drowning.

NEVER CO-SIGN a loan unless you're willing and able to pay off the entire debt. If your partner defaults, you're responsible for picking up the payments. If you don't, it will go into your credit report and you could be sued for collection, and your wages garnisheed.

Be an Early Bird.

YOU HAVE until April 15th of next year to invest in your IRA for this year, but the sooner you put in money the longer it has to grow on a tax-deferred basis.

Save Paper, Not Pennies.

As HOWARD HUGHES once said, "A million dollars is not what it used to be." Saving small change is no longer enough. Instead, put $3 a day plus all your change, seven days a week, in a jar and use it for something special. At the end of the year, you'll have well over a $1,000.

Skip Market-Timers.

ABOUT 75% of the recommendations made by market timing gurus underperform the strategy of buying and holding the S&P 500 Index.

— ¢ —

Piggyback on an Expert.

PICK A WELL-KNOWN, successful investor, such as Warren Buffet, Peter Lynch, or John Neff, and follow their recommendations, as reported in the media.

Check Social Security Records Every Three Years.

COMPARE YOUR W–2 withholding with the Social Security Administration's printout. Errors occur in over 5% of all accounts and an uncorrected mistake could cut your lifetime benefits.

Know Where the Fed Is.

GET THE address and telephone number of the nearest Federal Reserve Bank or branch from your phone book. All provide a range of free information, including details on how to buy no-fee Treasuries.

Take News with a Grain of Salt.

GOOD NEWS is often exaggerated. Bad news is often swept under the rug. Keep this in mind when investing.

Clip Coupons.

THE AVERAGE coupon is worth 85 cents. Use five a week and you'll save $221 in one year.

—¢ —

Save Your Overflow.

IF YOU'VE reached your maximum 401(k) contribution before the year is out, have your payroll department deposit enough money on a monthly basis for the rest of the year in your IRA so that by December 31st you'll have $2,000 in the account.

Hang in There.

YOUR PENSION benefits grow most during the last few years that you're working. Make sure any early retirement package is generous enough to cover benefits lost by leaving before you're 60 or 65.

Never Grocery Shop Without a List or When You're Hungry.

You'll END up with a pantry full of junk food.

— ¢ —

Know When Tax-free Pays Off.

To DETERMINE if a tax-free bond is worth buying, divide its yield by one, minus your tax bracket. This figure shows how much you need to earn from a taxable investment to get the same return. For example, a tax-free municipal bond yields 4%. You're in the 31% tax bracket. Divide 4% by 0.69 (1 minus 0.31). The result: 5.79%. In this case, a taxable investment would have to yield over 5.79% to give you more income than the tax-free bond.

Buy a Car in December.

AT YEAR'S end, auto dealers are desperate to empty their lots to make room for next year's models. Consequently, they slash prices.

Keep on Track.

BY THE time you're 50 you should have saved two times your annual earnings—in your retirement plan or with other investments.

Stay Put If You're Nearly Vested.

BEFORE LEAVING one job for another, find out how the move will affect your existing pension benefits. Federal law requires that employee benefits must be 100% vested (nonforfeitable) after five years of work or 20% vested after three and increased to 100% after seven years.

Line Up the Mortgage Before the House.

YOU'LL KNOW what you can afford. Then, spend 10% less.

— ¢ —

Don't Blow a Windfall.

IF YOU'RE lucky enough to get one, follow my "one-third" formula: use one-third for something special that you've always wanted, one-third for savings or IRA, and the balance for paying off a debt.

Don't Equate Marriage with Financial Advantage.

BEING MARRIED is not always better if you're collecting Social Security. As a single, you and your partner can each have an income of up to $25,000 before your benefits are subject to tax. If you marry and file jointly, that amount is reduced to just $32,000, and you'll have to forfeit your deceased spouse's Social Security benefits.

— ¢ —

Get Your Newborn a Social Security Number.

THIS WILL allow you to claim your child as a dependent on your tax return and to open an account in his/her name for savings bonds and other financial gifts.

Attempt Temping.

IF YOU'VE lost your job, look for temp work. It's no longer the sole province of receptionists and secretaries. Engineers, lawyers, chemists, executives, physicians, and others are all doing temp work—and 40% are eventually offered full-time positions. Many placement firms also provide paid vacations, sick days, retirement plans, and health insurance.

Negotiate Credit Card Interest.

IF YOU'VE made your payments on time for 12 consecutive months, call the card issuer and ask for a lower interest rate or lower annual fee. If you sense reluctance, threaten to switch to another card.

Buy a Car the Last Week of the Month.

SALESMEN ARE trying to meet their monthly quota, and bargains abound.

— ¢ —

Don't Just Pay the Minimum on Your Credit Card.

IF YOU do, you'll be in debt forever. Add something extra every month, even if it's only $20.

Bank Where Your Employer Banks.

YOU'LL HAVE more leverage when negotiating a loan, mortgage, and overdraft protection than at an institution where you're just a number.

— ¢ —

Steer Clear of Credit Doctors.

CREDIT REPAIR clinics charge hundreds of dollars and usually accomplish nothing. Use only a non-profit consumer foundation for help with credit card debt.

Update Your Will.

LIFE'S LITTLE changes quickly add up. Retirement, buying or selling property, coming into a financial windfall, the birth of a child or grandchild, death of a spouse, a move to a new state, marriage, divorce, a major change in health—all mean it's time for a revision.

Report Bad Grades.

IF YOU find disturbing information in your company's pension plan report, contact the local field office of the Department of Labor's Pension and Welfare Benefits Administration. They are the top watchdog group.

Don't Buy a Porsche If You Can't Afford to Insure It.

COVERAGE OF an expensive sports car runs three to four times more than on a standard model. Call your agent *before* buying a car and get the costs for several models.

Toss Out Low Yields.

As WILL ROGERS said, "Even if you're on the right track, you'll get run over if you just sit there." When a CD comes due, don't automatically roll it over into another. If you find a higher yield at another bank, in a money market fund, or with Treasuries, switch. Shop rates now so you'll be in the know when the time comes.

Make Friends with a Bank Officer.

INTRODUCE YOURSELF. Leave your business card. Keep in touch. It will pay off when you need a loan, quick service, or to straighten out a problem.

Remember That Charity Doesn't Always Begin at Home.

IT ALSO begins with common sense. Never give money to a fundraiser who says hundreds of children or animals will die within hours if you don't mail a check at once. Or to one who offers to send a messenger to your house or office to pick up your donation.

Sign Up for Tax-free Day Care.

IF YOU have a child under 13 (or a parent who is ill), enroll in a Flexible Spending Account at work. An FSA lets you set aside up to $5,000 of your before-tax salary in a special account and use it to pay for babysitters, day camp, before and after school programs, and adult care. You don't have to pay income tax on the amount you put in your FSA—but you do forfeit any amount that isn't spent during the year.

Prepay Your Mortgage.

ADD JUST $25 more a month to your mortgage check. On a 30-year, 8% fixed rate mortgage, you'll save $23,337 over the life of the loan. Prepay $100 a month and you'll save about $62,000 in interest. Aim to be mortgage-free before you retire. The last thing you need when you're on a set income are monthly mortgage payments.

Set Aside Money for Domestic Help Throughout the Year.

COME APRIL 15th, you'll owe an entire year's worth of Social Security taxes for any household help you paid $1,000 or more for during the year. The tax is 7.56% of wages.

Sell on the News, Buy on the Sly.

ONCE A STOCK is in the news, everyone knows about it. To make a Wall Street killing, buy little-known, rarely followed, undiscovered but smart companies.

Go for Preferreds.

BUY A-RATED preferred stocks for very safe, very high guaranteed yields. They are identified by the letters "pf" in the stock listings.

— ¢ —

Never Doubt the Fed.

THE FEDERAL Reserve Board determines the direction interest rates take and, to some extent, the severity of inflation. Watch what the Fed is doing and invest accordingly.

Learn from Your Mistakes.

THEY HAPPEN—even to the most seasoned investors. Don't bury your head in the sand when you make one. Profit from the experience.

Spend as Much Time Researching a Stock or Mutual Fund as You Would a New Car or Computer.

IN OTHER words, do your homework.

Don't Protect Your Clunker.

DROP COLLISION coverage on an older car if your premium is equal to 10% or more of the value of the car. You'll save a bundle. Collision covers the cost of repairing your car if you're in an accident. But, for older cars, coverage is often higher than the actual repair costs.

Don't Put Yourself in a Hole.

OVERSPENDING MEANS that your future earnings are already spoken for.

— ¢ —

Never Add Charges to a Credit Card with an Outstanding Balance.

BECAUSE THERE'S no grace period, interest begins to accumulate immediately.

Think Back to the Year B.C.—
Before Credit.

PEOPLE LIKE your parents or grandparents actually went through life using checks or cash. It worked then and it works now. Do the same and you'll wind up spending 20% to 45% less.

Reduce Your Credit Card Limit.

JUST BECAUSE the issuer increases your limit doesn't mean you have to increase your balance. Ask that it be lowered to an amount you can handle.

Stop Junk Mail.

UNSOLICITED CATALOGS are full of temptations to spend. Call the company to remove your name from its list. Your mail carrier will be grateful, too.

Roll Over Bank CDs If Rates Are High.

INVEST IN certificates with different maturity dates: six months, one year, five years. When each CD matures, roll it over into another if rates are high. Otherwise, put it into your money market fund. This is called "laddering."

— ¢ —

Go Veggie.

ELIMINATING MEAT from your life is good for your health and good for your budget.

Live Within Your Means.

SOMEONE ELSE will always have more expensive toys.

— ¢ —

Pad Your IRA.

HAVE YOUR mutual fund transfer $38.50 per week from your checking account into your IRA. Within twelve months you'll have the max you can put in your IRA—$2,000—without missing a bit of it.

Remodel Before You Move.

IF YOU plan to sell your house one day, do makeovers that will pay you back. In descending order of cost-effectiveness: a new kitchen, new bathroom, new family room, and new master suite. Other worthwhile projects: renovating an attic, adding a deck, and replacing drafty windows.

Let Your Home Equity Pay for College.

COLLEGES DO not consider home equity a family asset when allocating financial aid. After financial aid is awarded, take out a home equity loan to pay for remaining college costs. The interest will be tax deductible.

Dump Your PMI.

LENDERS REQUIRE that you buy Private Mortgage Insurance (PMI) if you put less than 20% down on a new house. As soon as you've built up over 80% equity in the house, cancel the PMI—it's expensive.

Keep Track of Small Things That Might Be Tax Deductible.

SOME ITEMS to track: automobile expenses for volunteer activities; job search expenses in the same line of work, including resumé costs and travel to and from interviews; union and professional dues; job-related uniforms and their upkeep; tax preparation fees; fair market value of clothing donated to charity; calls to your stockbroker (but never on Monday, please); subscriptions to investment magazines; fees for safe deposit boxes used to hold stock certificates and other investment items; and, of course, the price of this book.

Protect Your Money Before Your Children Apply for College.

ASSETS IN an IRA and/or other qualified retirement plans are not considered in the college aid formula.

— ¢ —

Never Pay a Fee for Buying Treasuries.

U.S. TREASURY bills, notes, and bonds can be purchased directly from Federal Reserve Banks and their branches. So why pay a broker to buy them for you? Consult the phone book for the nearest Federal Reserve bank.

Never Pay a Contractor in Full Up Front.

GET A FINAL, total price in writing that includes time and cost of materials. Pay in stages as the job is being done, holding out 20% until the work is completed to your satisfaction. Never pay for materials until they're actually delivered.

Direct Deposit Your Tax Refund into Savings.

FILL OUT IRS Form 8888, which is attached to your 1040 or 1040A. You'll get your refund faster and you won't be as tempted to spend it.

Put Savings Bonds in Your Name.

IF YOU'RE going to use EE bonds for your child's college tuition, register them in your name. EE bonds won't escape federal taxes if they're in your child's name. (This tax break applies only to families within certain income levels.)

Get an IRA—Even If You Don't Qualify for the Tax Deduction.

CONTRIBUTE $2,000 annually to a nondeductible IRA and you'll accumulate $297,200 after 30 years, compared with $183,300 in a taxable account, assuming it earns 9% annually and you're in the 28% tax bracket.

Keep Jewelry in Your Safe Deposit Box.

You'll reduce the cost of insurance.

— ¢ —

Have Your Kids Take College Courses in High School.

Eliminating one college course can save at least $600. (They'll need to attend a college that charges by the credit, not by the semester—most likely a state school.)

Buy Treasuries If the Stock Market Scares You.

U.S. TREASURIES are as safe as bank CDs and money market funds, usually pay higher returns, and are free of state and local income taxes.

Get an Umbrella.

IF YOU own a house, have other major assets, or serve on a nonprofit board, buy an umbrella liability policy. It protects you from financial loss above your property/casualty coverage in case you're sued for damages. Just $150 to $300 per year buys you up to $1 million in coverage.

Don't Regard All Interest as Equal.

INTEREST ON a home mortgage or a home equity line of credit on your principal residence and one other house is generally tax deductible. Interest paid on car or credit card loans is not.

Enter Credit Card Purchases in Your Checkbook.

THIS RUNNING tally of how much you're spending lets you know whether you really can afford that next purchase.

Use Only Your Bank's ATM Network.

MOST BANKS charge up to $3 for each transaction posted at an ATM in a different network.

Ease Up on the AC.

SET YOUR air conditioner at 78 degrees, not at 72. You'll cut warm weather energy costs by up to 39%.

— ¢ —

Know When to Say Hello.

THE MOST expensive block of time to use the telephone is from 8 A.M. to 5 P.M. Monday through Friday. The cheapest time— 11 P.M. to 8 A.M. every day—gets you a 65% discount.

Join AARP.

IF YOU'RE **50** years of age or older, join the American Association of Retired Persons. Members get a **10%** to **30%** discount at nearly every hotel or motel and on car rentals. Take AARP's "55 Alive" mature driver refresher course and cut your auto insurance costs.

Order Medication by Mail.

Discount mail-order services sell drugs for 10% to 35% less than your neighborhood drugstore.

Complain.

IF YOU have trouble with a product, most companies will refund your money or send you a coupon for a replacement. Look for the toll-free number on the product label.

Don't Panic Out of the Market.

LOSSES IN the 1987 stock market collapse were fully recovered within one year.

Don't Overspend on Special Events.

DON'T LET emotions blow your budget. Weddings, christenings, birthdays, and anniversaries usually lead to overspending. Avoid the trap.

Reduce Your Capital Gains Taxes.

BE TAX efficient. Hold onto winning mutual funds and stocks, but sell losers to get a tax loss. You can deduct up to $3,000 of investment losses in any one year against your ordinary income. If you have more than $3,000 in losses, the IRS lets you carry that amount over to the following year.

Save Up to 50% on Hotels.

CALL THE convention & visitor's bureau in the city you plan to visit for a list of discount hotel rates. Deals are seasonal, so check regularly. Usually, kids sleep free in the same room with their parents, seniors get reduced rates, and weekend packages are generally lower than weekday prices.

Go Beyond Your IRA and 401(k).

IF YOU'VE contributed the maximum to your IRA and 401(k), buy an A-rated annuity. Money invested in an annuity will grow on a tax-deferred basis until withdrawn—after you turn 59½. Unlike IRAs, Keoghs, and 401(k)s, there's no ceiling on the dollar amount you can contribute.

Give It Away.

ANYONE CAN give up to $10,000 per recipient per year, free of gift tax. A couple can jointly give $20,000—a great strategy for reducing the size of your taxable estate without paying a lawyer.

Beware of Mutual Funds Sold by Banks.

THEY ARE not necessarily insured by the FDIC.

225

Don't Take It with You.

LOWER FUNERAL expenses for your survivors by requesting an inexpensive casket in writing. Funeral homes rarely have them on display—probably because they start at about $300, versus $1,000 for an elegant version.

Never Call Your Bank.

AT LEAST not until you know what the charge is. Many banks sock customers with fees ($3 on average) for information— even for simple balance inquiries.

—¢—

Keep Home Improvement Receipts.

NO MATTER how small. When you sell your home, add these expenses to the cost basis—the figure used to determine a gain or loss on your house. Improvements made over the years can add up to thousands of dollars in tax savings.

Put It in Writing.

ALL LOAN agreements, even those between family and friends, should include the interest rate and repayment schedule. If you don't charge interest, the IRS may regard the loan as a gift. If so, the loan will be subject to taxes.

Get Home Insurance—
Even If You Rent.

TAKE OUT a policy that covers at least 80% of the replacement cost of your possessions. If you have a computer, fax, or other office equipment in your home, get a home office rider. If you're a party giver, get a "host liquor" rider added to your policy to protect you against lawsuits from those who, after leaving your place, have an alcohol-related accident.

Buy a Used Rental Car or Demonstration Model.

YOU'LL SAVE 15% to 20% and pay less insurance than with a new car. Get a copy of the maintenance record first and then negotiate a warranty.

Buy a Car That's Overstocked.

AUTO DEALERS inevitably offer cash rebates on these models.

230

Lower Your Homeowner's Insurance.

INSTALL A SMOKE detector, burglar alarm, and deadbolt locks. Get a long-term policy. Use the same insurer for three to five years and reduce your premiums by 5%. Stick with an agent for six years or more and you'll get a 10% discount.

Subscribe to Magazines.

IF YOU know you're going to buy a newsstand copy of a particular magazine every week or month, subscribe. It's much cheaper than purchasing individual copies. Use it for investment advice and it's tax deductible. So is this book!

— ¢ —

Pump Your Own Gas.

YOU'LL SAVE about 10 cents per gallon.

Bypass the Babysitter.

SET UP a co-op service with family and friends to save money.

Skip Shopping Malls When You Feel Blue.

Depression often triggers a spending spree. Instead, take a walk, call a friend, or go to a movie.

Dine Out for a Reason.

SAVE RESTAURANTS for special occasions. Put a weekly or monthly limit on how often you'll abandon your own kitchen at dinner time.

— ¢ —

Skip the Before and After.

YOU'LL SAVE a quarter of the price of dinner if you bypass the appetizer or dessert. You'll also save on calories.

Use a Discount Dining Card.

IT WILL save you 20% to 30% off your restaurant bill.

— ¢ —

Don't Buy "Pre-".

PRECUT, PREPARED, prechopped, presliced, and prepackaged items at the grocery store are always more expensive.

Steer Clear of Convenience Stores.

UNLESS IT'S midnight or an emergency, drive by. Prices are ridiculously high on most items.

Get Disability Insurance.

ACCIDENTS ARE never planned, but you should plan for them. Get a policy that can't be canceled, has a residual benefit rider that lets you work part time or in a lower paying job, and provides "own occupation" coverage so you'll receive money if you're unable to perform your regular job. Buy coverage for 60% to 80% of your income.

Buy a House in the Best School District You Can Afford.

FOLLOW THIS strategy whether or not you have school-age children. Resale values of homes in good school districts are always higher.

Don't Be a Switch-hitter.

EACH TIME you apply for a new credit card, the issuer takes a look at your credit file, adding what's known as an "inquiry notice" to your report. Too many inquiries (five or six) over a short time means you could be seen as a credit risk to future lenders.

Don't Open a "Uniform Gift to Minor" Account.

IF YOU think your child may qualify for financial aid, don't put money in his name. Thirty-five percent of a student's own money is counted toward the expected contribution to tuition. The larger his account, the smaller his "need" for financial aid.

Live Like One When You Expect to Be Three.

IF YOU and your partner are expecting your first child, start to save one salary and live on the other. That's how it will be, at least for a while, after the baby arrives.

Sign Up for COBRA.

THE CONGRESSIONAL Omnibus Budget Reconciliation Act (COBRA) allows you to continue your group health insurance coverage after you lose or leave your job. But it's up to you to fill out the forms. If you leave voluntarily, coverage is provided for 18 months; if you are disabled, for 29 months; in the event of widowhood, divorce or company bankruptcy, for 36 months.

Never Call Your Broker on Monday.

OUT OF courtesy and common sense, wait until Tuesday. A good broker is focused on the opening of the market—at home and around the world—and on getting back into a business frame of mind after the weekend.